ALTERNATIVE ENERGY

NUCLEAR
ENERGY

by Meg Marquardt

D0125744

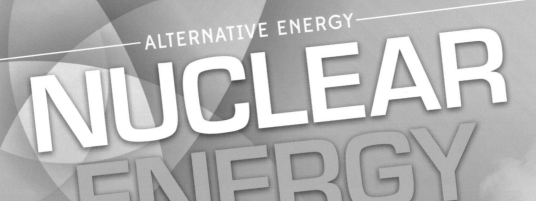

Content Consultant
Andrew Kadak
Past President of the American Nuclear Society
Past Professor of the Practice
MIT Nuclear Science and Engineering Department

Core Library

An Imprint of Abdo Publishing
abdopublishing.com

abdopublishing.com

Published by Abdo Publishing, a division of ABDO, PO Box 398166, Minneapolis, Minnesota 55439. Copyright © 2017 by Abdo Consulting Group, Inc. International copyrights reserved in all countries. No part of this book may be reproduced in any form without written permission from the publisher. Core Library™ is a trademark and logo of Abdo Publishing.

Printed in the United States of America, North Mankato, Minnesota
092016
012017

THIS BOOK CONTAINS RECYCLED MATERIALS

Cover Photo: R. Classen/Shutterstock Images
Interior Photos: R. Classen/Shutterstock Images, 1; US Navy, 4, 45; Kopytin Georgy/Shutterstock Images, 7; Denton Rumsey/Shutterstock Images, 9, 43; Science Source, 12; Popperfoto/Getty Images, 15; AP Images, 17, 18; Roman Sigaev/Shutterstock Images, 22; Ned Haines/Science Source, 25; SPL/Science Source, 27; James King-Holmes/Science Source, 29; Dorling Kindersley/Thinkstock, 31 (top), 31 (bottom); Enrico Sacchetti/Science Source, 32; Shutterstock Images, 34; Novosti/Science Source, 37; Thomas Kienzle/AP Images, 38

Editor: Arnold Ringstad
Series Designer: Nikki Farinella

Publisher's Cataloging-in-Publication Data

Names: Marquardt, Meg, author.
Title: Nuclear energy / by Meg Marquardt.
Description: Minneapolis, MN : Abdo Publishing, 2017. | Series: Alternative energy | Includes bibliographical references and index.
Identifiers: LCCN 2016945412 | ISBN 9781680784572 (lib. bdg.) | ISBN 9781680798425 (ebook)
Subjects: LCSH: Nuclear energy--Juvenile literature. | Renewable energy sources--Juvenile literature.
Classification: DDC 621.48--dc23
LC record available at http://lccn.loc.gov/2016945412

CONTENTS

CHAPTER ONE
Powered by Nuclear Energy . . . 4

CHAPTER TWO
The History of Nuclear Power . .12

CHAPTER THREE
**The Science of
Fission and Fusion** 22

CHAPTER FOUR
A Bright Future 34

Fast Facts 42

Stop and Think 44

Glossary 46

Learn More 47

Index 48

About the Author 48

POWERED BY NUCLEAR ENERGY

The nuclear submarine has been underwater for a month. It is stalking a rival sub. The second sub is powered by diesel fuel. It needs fresh air to run its engine. It must surface every few weeks. But the first sub has a nuclear reactor. It does not need air. It can stay underwater as long as it needs to. The submarine can remain hidden in the depths of the ocean.

Submarines that use nuclear power can travel for years without refueling.

Inside the reactor is fuel made of uranium. The reactor splits uranium atoms apart. This process is called fission. The reaction creates heat. Water flows past the heat source. It boils and turns to steam. Steam then powers the whole ship. The nuclear reactor works for years without refueling. The limiting factor is the crew. They need food and other supplies. If a nuclear sub did not need a crew, it could stay underwater for 25 years.

An Alternative Energy Source

Today most of the world's energy comes from fossil fuels. These are made up of the remains of prehistoric plants and animals. These fuels are

USS *Nautilus*

The world's first nuclear submarine was the USS *Nautilus*. The US Navy launched it on January 21, 1954. The sub beat speed and distance records. It was the first to cross under the icy North Pole. Researchers learned a lot from it. They soon built even better ships. The *Nautilus* was declared a national historical landmark. It later became a museum. Visitors can tour it in Groton, Connecticut.

Coal is one of the most widely used fossil fuels.

commonly found underground. Burning them releases energy. Major fossil fuels include oil, coal, and natural gas. Gasoline powers most of the cars now on the road. It is made from oil.

Fossil fuels have important downsides. There is only a limited amount of them available. Someday they will run out. They also harm the environment. Fossil fuels are burned to produce energy. The burning process releases greenhouse gases. These can lead to climate change. Nuclear energy lacks these downsides. It is one of many alternatives to fossil fuels.

The Fuel of Tomorrow?

In submarines, nuclear reactors provide energy to move the sub. On land, reactors generate electricity. Since the 1950s, power companies have used them as a source of clean energy.

However, nuclear energy also has downsides. Nuclear reactions can be dangerous if they get out of control. These accidents are very rare. Only three major ones have happened in the history of nuclear power. Waste products are another downside. Reactors create waste that remains dangerous for a long time. It stays radioactive for thousands of years.

Nuclear power plants often have large cooling towers that are much larger than the actual reactor, found in the smaller rounded structure.

Nuclear Power in Space

Submarines are not the only vehicles that use nuclear power. Since the 1950s, researchers have studied ways to use it in space. Some projects involve using nuclear reactors to power rockets. These designs have never flown in space. However, one type of nuclear power has been used in spacecraft. Many robotic probes have small radioisotope thermoelectric generators. These devices create electricity from heat given off by radioactive elements. The Mars rover *Curiosity* uses this type of power. So does the *New Horizons* probe that visited Pluto in 2015.

Scientists are seeking ways to store it safely.

Researchers have made reactors smaller and safer. They are working on new advances. One is a nuclear reaction called fusion. Fusion combines atoms rather than splitting them. It may be safer than fission. However, there are many technical challenges to overcome before fusion reactors can be used.

Nuclear power's history is long. It involves many breakthroughs. It began when scientists discovered atoms and radiation. Many years later, engineers built the first nuclear power plant. Nuclear researchers continue improving this energy source. They hope it will power our future.

FURTHER EVIDENCE

This chapter introduces the benefits and drawbacks of nuclear energy. What was one of the main points of this chapter? What evidence was used to support this point? The website below contains more information about nuclear power. Does the information on the website support the main point of the chapter? Does it present new evidence?

Nuclear Energy Institute
mycorelibrary.com/nuclear-energy

CHAPTER TWO

THE HISTORY OF NUCLEAR POWER

The story of nuclear power begins with the discovery of radiation. In 1896 physicist Henri Becquerel tried to make X-ray images. He planned to use sunlight as an energy source. The day turned out to be cloudy. But he tried the experiment anyway. The X-rays still showed up.

That meant the energy was not coming from the sun. Becquerel was using photographic plates

Henri Becquerel's lab was one of the earliest places where radiation research was performed.

that contained uranium. He had thought the sunlight provided energy to the uranium. Then this energy would make the X-ray images. But sunlight was not present. That meant the uranium was giving off energy itself. This energy was radioactivity.

Other scientists began to experiment with radioactivity. One of them was Marie Curie. She found that certain natural elements gave off radiation. It did not seem to matter which form one of these elements was in. The element could be a crystal or a powder. Radiation was still detected.

Marie Curie and Pitchblende

Getting radioactive material is not easy. Curie used pitchblende as a source of radioactive elements. Pitchblende was an expensive ore. Once Curie had it, she had to separate the radioactive elements. This was a difficult process. It required many rounds of chemical reactions. She started with thousands of pounds of pitchblende. After three years she had 0.004 ounces (0.1 g) of a radioactive substance.

Marie Curie and her husband, Pierre, made important discoveries in the field of radioactivity.

Curie realized the radiation came from inside the element itself. She was observing the natural process of radioactive decay.

From Atoms to a Bomb

Marie's discovery inspired more research. Others began hunting for the source of this mysterious energy. They realized that radiation involved protons and neutrons. These particles are found at the center of an atom. Some atoms are unstable. Particles may be ejected from them. This process is known as radioactive decay. When decay happens, energy is released.

Researchers tried to harness radioactive decay. By 1939 German physicists learned how to split a uranium atom. They did this by hitting it with neutrons. Soon after, the United States began the Manhattan Project. The goal of this secret program was to build an atomic bomb. The program succeeded. The United States dropped two atomic bombs on Japanese cities to help end

The atomic bombs dropped on Japan showed the power of out-of-control fission.

President Dwight Eisenhower envisioned peaceful uses for nuclear power.

World War II (1939–1945). The bombs used fission to cause death and devastation. They showed the dangerous power nuclear reactions could unleash.

Clean Energy

After the war, researchers looked for peaceful ways to use nuclear power. President Dwight Eisenhower called for an "Atoms for Peace" program. The program sped up nuclear research. Scientists already knew nuclear fission could produce power. They also knew it could be dangerous. If the reaction ran out of control, it could happen too quickly. It could generate too much heat and destroy a power plant. Still, nuclear power seemed like the energy source of the future.

By 1957 the first commercial nuclear reactor was ready for testing. The technology was based on reactors in submarines. The reactor contained nuclear fuel. The rate of fission could be sped up or slowed. Neutron-absorbing control rods were used to do this. If necessary, the rods

Radioactive Isotopes

Radioactive elements used in nuclear power are called radioactive isotopes. They are also known as radioisotopes. Isotopes are versions of elements that contain varying numbers of neutrons. They shed energy in the form of radiation. This shedding process is radioactive decay.

could be inserted to completely stop the reaction. A reactor in Pennsylvania became the first nuclear reactor to generate electricity for homes.

More than 50 years have passed since the first reactor went online. By 2016 there were more than 400 nuclear reactors worldwide. They produced approximately 11 percent of the world's electricity. In some countries, reactors are controversial. Many people are unwilling to accept nuclear power. They feel its risks and dangers are too high. Many scientists disagree. They say nuclear power has proven to be very safe.

A group of climate scientists wrote a letter to environmental organizations that oppose nuclear power. The scientists encouraged them to change their minds:

> *As climate and energy scientists concerned with global climate change, we are writing to urge you to advocate the development and deployment of safer nuclear energy systems. We appreciate your organization's concern about global warming, and your advocacy of renewable energy. But continued opposition to nuclear power threatens humanity's ability to avoid dangerous climate change.*
>
> Source: *"Top Climate Change Scientists' Letter to Policy Influencers." CNN. CNN, November 3, 2013. Web. Accessed June 29, 2016.*

What's the Big Idea?

The scientists take a strong stance on the connection between nuclear power and climate change. What is their main point?

THE SCIENCE OF FISSION AND FUSION

Nuclear power comes in two main forms: fission and fusion. Fission involves splitting atoms apart. Fusion involves smashing them together. Fission reactors already exist. Researchers are still working on creating a fusion reactor. Fission reactors create clean energy, but they have drawbacks. Fusion reactors would lack many of these

Reactions happening at the tiny scale of atoms make nuclear energy possible.

drawbacks. However, they are much more difficult to make.

Nuclear Fission

Atoms usually do not naturally split apart. But under certain conditions they become unstable. One of these conditions is the addition of extra neutrons. Neutrons are found in all atoms except for hydrogen atoms. When there are too many neutrons, an atom gets rid of the extra ones. This is when fission happens.

Nuclear reactors are full of two types of uranium isotopes. They are called U-238 and U-235. Their numbers represent the total number of neutrons and protons in each atom. U-235 is unstable.

Other Uses for Radiation

Radiation is not used only in nuclear power. It is used in medicine as a cancer treatment. Radiation is also used to kill dangerous bacteria in food products. It helps make some meats and vegetables safe to eat.

Major uranium mines are found in Australia, Kazakhstan, and Canada.

It naturally undergoes radioactive decay. In a nuclear reactor, scientists make it even more unstable. Neutrons produced in the reactor hit uranium atoms in the fuel. Those extra neutrons break U-235 apart. As it splits, it releases even more neutrons. These neutrons hit other uranium atoms. They split too. This process is called a chain reaction. Extra neutrons also strike the U-238. This creates the isotope U-239. U-239 decays into Plutonium-239. This element can then undergo fission in the reactor.

Neutrons are not the only things released when an atom splits. A lot of heat is also released. That heat warms up water into steam. That steam spins a turbine. A generator turns this motion into electricity.

Chain reactions are carefully controlled. But dangers still exist. If there is not enough water to cool the fuel, the fuel can overheat and melt. Additionally, the used fuel is dangerously radioactive. In some countries, this waste is recycled to create new fuel. Elsewhere, people store it in safe locations.

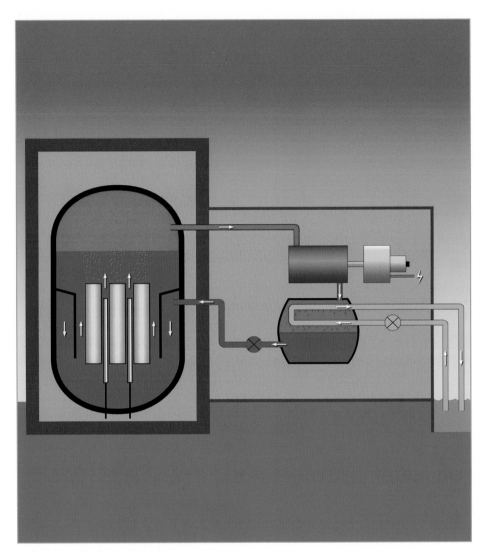

Inside a Fission Reactor

A nuclear reactor is a complicated piece of technology. But its main goal is simple. It creates heat and makes steam. Nuclear fission creates lots of heat. That heat is created in the core of the reactor, *yellow*. Water, *blue*, flows through this area. That water heats up. It boils and turns to steam, *red*. The steam then powers a turbine, *green*. The turbine makes electricity using a generator, *grey*. How does this diagram help you better understand the process behind nuclear energy?

The Fukushima Disaster

In 2011 a huge earthquake struck near Japan. A giant tsunami then slammed into the country. The rushing waters hit the Fukushima Daiichi nuclear power plant. The tsunami flooded the plant, disabling many safety systems. The fuel overheated and melted. The reactor was eventually controlled. However, explosions damaged the building. Radiation was released into the area. Nearby communities were evacuated. The Fukushima disaster was a reminder that safety measures can fail. Nuclear plants must be strongly protected against natural disasters.

Nuclear Fusion

Unlike fission, nuclear fusion does not split atoms. The opposite happens. In fusion, two atoms of hydrogen combine. Fusion does not rely on radioactive decay. Hydrogen is not radioactive. That means less radioactive waste is created. There is also no threat of a meltdown.

However, fusion is hard to achieve. It requires overcoming a major hurdle. To make fusion happen, two positively charged atoms have to be forced together.

Scientists and engineers around the world are working to develop fusion reactors.

Most of the time, atoms with positive charges push apart from each other. This force is very strong. The trick is to get atoms moving fast enough. Under high temperatures, atoms move extremely fast. The temperatures needed are as high as those on the sun. Eventually, the atoms move fast enough that they cannot stop from colliding together. At certain speeds, two atoms can crash into each other. They fuse into a single atom. When atoms fuse they give off large amounts of energy. This is the process that powers the sun.

But fusion reactors need a lot of energy to start the reaction. Right now, no fusion reactor creates more energy than it takes to start the process in the first place. This makes the process impractical for use in power plants. It is one of many challenges that fusion researchers face.

However, new developments may make fusion the nuclear power of the future. It produces less radioactive waste than fission. It also uses more

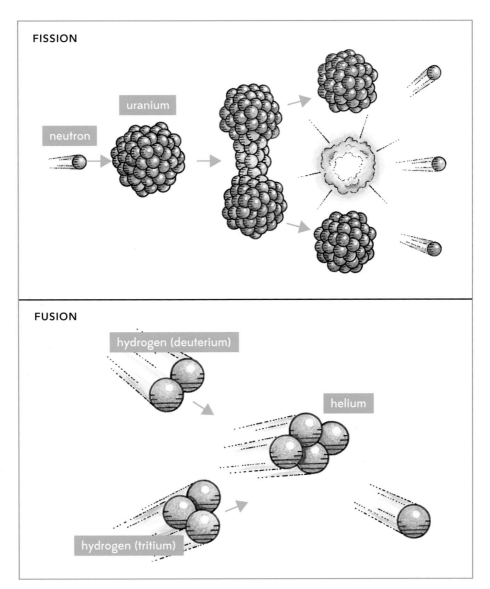

FISSION

neutron

uranium

FUSION

hydrogen (deuterium)

helium

hydrogen (tritium)

Fission and Fusion

Fission and fusion work in very different ways. In fission, an atom is hit with neutrons. Those neutrons knock other neutrons out of uranium atoms. This splits the atoms apart and creates a burst of energy. In fusion, two types of hydrogen atoms are forced to come together. They release energy as they fuse. How does the diagram help you understand the two different reaction processes?

Researchers are studying how to contain the amazingly hot material, called plasma, that would exist within fusion reactors.

common elements, such as hydrogen. If scientists can solve fusion's problems, they might have the perfect power source for a clean energy future.

EXPLORE ONLINE

Chapter Three discusses the science behind nuclear fission and fusion. The website below includes more information about this subject. How is the information on the website below presented differently from the information in this book? What new information can you learn from this website?

Nuclear Fission and Fusion
mycorelibrary.com/nuclear-energy

CHAPTER FOUR

A BRIGHT FUTURE

While nuclear submarines became a reality, many other vehicles did not. In the 1950s, the United States looked into nuclear-powered planes. They were not built. Nuclear reactors are unlikely to end up in planes or cars. However, they can help power cars indirectly. Electric cars are becoming more popular. Owners charge their cars' batteries using available

Electric cars can use nuclear power as their source of electricity.

electricity sources. These are often fossil fuel power plants. Nuclear power plants can provide this electricity too. And they can do it without creating harmful pollution.

Environmental Issues

Nuclear power can have a positive effect on the environment. In parts of the world, countries use nuclear power plants to desalinate water. Desalination is the process of removing salt from seawater. That makes it drinkable.

However, environmental risks still exist. Nuclear meltdowns are extremely unlikely. Only a few have ever happened. But when they do happen, they are serious problems. A nuclear meltdown could contaminate a region for decades. Researchers must figure out how to quickly and safely clean up nuclear accidents.

Nuclear waste remains radioactive for hundreds of thousands of years. That means it has to be stored safely for that long. But figuring out where to store it

An explosion at the Chernobyl nuclear power plant in Ukraine in 1986 released dangerous radiation to nearby areas.

Workers store nuclear waste at temporary sites while scientists and politicians find acceptable permanent locations.

has led to disputes. Many local communities do not want this waste stored nearby. This is a challenge that researchers and politicians have yet to overcome.

Looking Ahead

Despite these challenges, there is still hope for nuclear power. The fact remains that the world needs to find new forms of energy. Fossil fuels are not renewable. They will eventually run out. Nuclear power is one option to replace them.

Even the problem of nuclear waste might be overcome. Scientists are working on fusion reactors. If they succeed, people could power

Yucca Mountain

One proposed storage site for nuclear waste was Yucca Mountain in Nevada. This was part of the Nevada Test Site. Nuclear weapons were once tested there. In 1987 the US government decided to store nuclear waste at Yucca Mountain. But in 2010, concerns from the public and politicians led to the end of the plan. By 2016 the United States still had no long-term storage plan in place. Most nuclear power plants simply store their waste at the plant itself.

Detecting Radiation

Radiation is invisible. It can be hard to detect without special equipment. However, millions of people already have potential radiation detectors in their pockets: smartphones. Researchers discovered that some smartphone camera sensors can detect radiation sources. This technology could be useful for first responders who arrive at accidents involving radiation.

Earth in the same way the sun powers itself. Such a breakthrough could change the future of energy technology forever. Smashing together atoms of hydrogen may make it possible to create clean energy lasting thousands of years for the entire world.

In an interview, physics professor Martin Hoffert discussed one possibility for the future of fusion technology:

> *I think we'll eventually be successful with fusion, but we need to have different systems and perhaps different fuels. One of the fuels now being considered instead of tritium is a helium isotope called helium-3. It would have a lot of advantages in a fusion power plant, because it wouldn't make the walls of the reactor radioactive. Unfortunately, there isn't much helium-3 on the Earth, though it turns out that the Apollo astronauts found helium-3 on the moon in concentrations that might be economically recoverable. If fusion reactors that rely on helium-3 could be made to work, then even at the very high costs of launching materials into space and recovering them, it may be marginally cost-effective to get helium-3 from the moon.*

> Source: "Beyond Fossil Fuels." NOVA Frontline. *PBS, 2000.*
> *Web. Accessed June 29, 2016.*

Consider Your Audience

Adapt Hoffert's answer in your own words for a different audience, such as your classmates or a younger brother or sister. How would you explain the fusion process? How does your essay differ from Hoffert's original answer?

FAST FACTS

- Nuclear reactors are used in ships and in nuclear power plants.
- Scientists, including Marie Curie, have studied radiation and its effects since the late 1800s.
- In the 1940s, the United States developed and used atomic bombs. After the end of World War II in 1945, scientists researched how to use nuclear reactions for peaceful purposes.
- The first commercial nuclear power reactor was ready for testing in 1957.
- There are two major types of nuclear power. One is fission, and the other is fusion.
- Fission involves splitting atoms apart. It is used in all of today's working nuclear reactors.
- Fusion involves smashing atoms together. Scientists have not yet developed an efficient fusion reactor.
- Fission reactors create dangerous radioactive waste. Deciding where and how to store this waste has become a controversial issue.

- Nuclear power plants do not create the kinds of pollution generated by fossil fuel power plants.
- Meltdowns and other nuclear power plant accidents are extremely unlikely. However, if they do happen they have the potential to cause major damage to people and the environment.
- If scientists can perfect fusion reactor technology, these reactors may be even safer than today's fission versions.

Take a Stand

Nuclear power is a controversial subject. Some think that it is too dangerous to use. Others think that it is a clean, safe way to produce energy. Look back through the book. What is your opinion on this issue? Should people continue using nuclear power? Why or why not?

Why Do I Care?

Maybe there isn't a nuclear power plant near where you live. But that does not mean you cannot think about how these power plants affect the world. What benefits might a nuclear power plant bring to a city? What downsides might it bring? Would you want to live near one of these plants?

You Are There

This book discusses traveling in a nuclear submarine. Imagine you are a member of a nuclear submarine crew. You spend weeks at a time under the sea. Write a letter home talking about your adventures. What is it like spending so much time underwater? Be sure to add plenty of detail to your notes.

Dig Deeper

After reading this book, what questions do you still have about nuclear power? With an adult's help, find a few reliable sources that can help you answer your questions. Write a paragraph about what you learned.

GLOSSARY

fission
the splitting apart of heavy atoms, such as uranium

fossil fuels
fuels such as coal, oil, and natural gas that come from the remains of ancient plants and animals

fusion
the forcing of two light atoms of hydrogen to combine

greenhouse gases
gases that trap the sun's heat in the atmosphere, leading to climate change

isotope
a version of an element containing varying numbers of neutrons

meltdown
an event that occurs when a nuclear reactor overheats and melts the fuel

neutron
a particle in an atom that has no electric charge

proton
a particle in an atom that has a positive electric charge

radioactive decay
the process by which an atom loses particles, causing it to become a different kind of atom

turbine
a machine with a wheel or fan that generates electricity by spinning

LEARN MORE

Books

Marquardt, Meg. *The Science of a Nuclear Plant Explosion*. Ann Arbor, MI: Cherry Lake Publishing, 2016.

Ollhoff, Jim. *Nuclear Energy*. Minneapolis, MN: Abdo Publishing, 2010.

Rowell, Rebecca. *Marie Curie Advances the Study of Radioactivity*. Minneapolis, MN: Abdo Publishing, 2016.

Websites

To learn more about Alternative Energy, visit **booklinks.abdopublishing.com**. These links are routinely monitored and updated to provide the most current information available.

Visit **mycorelibrary.com** for free additional tools for teachers and students.

INDEX

atomic bombs, 16–18

Becquerel, Henri, 13–14

climate change, 8, 21
Curie, Marie, 14–16

Eisenhower, Dwight, 18–19
electric cars, 35–36

fossil fuels, 6–8, 36, 39
Fukushima Daiichi nuclear power plant, 28

greenhouse gases, 8

Hoffert, Martin, 41

isotopes, 10, 19, 24, 26, 41

meltdowns, 28, 36

Nautilus, USS, 6
nuclear fission, 6, 10, 18–19, 23–27, 31
nuclear fusion, 10, 23, 28–33, 39–40, 41
nuclear reactors, 5–6, 8, 10, 19–20, 23–27, 28, 30, 35, 39, 41
nuclear waste, 8, 26, 28, 30, 36–39

plutonium, 26

spacecraft, 10
submarines, 5–6, 8, 10, 19, 35

uranium, 6, 14, 16, 24, 26, 31

World War II, 16–18

X-rays, 13–14

Yucca Mountain, 39

ABOUT THE AUTHOR

Meg Marquardt started as a scientist but decided she liked writing about science even more. She enjoys researching physics, geology, and climate science. She lives in Madison, Wisconsin, with her two scientist cats, Lagrange and Doppler.